A KID'S GUIDE TO THE
Games™

MOTOCROSS

in the
Games

CHRISTOPHER BLOMQUIST

The Rosen Publishing Group's
PowerKids Press™
New York

For two Xtremely wonderful nephews, Timothy and James

Safety gear, including knee-high plastic boots, chest protectors, nylon pants, and a full-face helmet designed specifically for motocross, should be worn while riding motocross. Do not attempt tricks without proper gear, instruction, and supervision.

Published in 2003 by The Rosen Publishing Group, Inc.
29 East 21st Street, New York, NY 10010

First Edition.

Editor: Nancy MacDonell Smith
Book Design: Michael de Guzman and Mike Donnellan
Layout: Nick Sciacca

Photo Credits: Cover, pp. 4, 7, 12, 16, 19 © Icon Sports Media; pp. 8, 11 © Tony Donaldson/Icon SMI; p. 15 © Jed Jacobsohn/Getty Images; p. 21 © Al Berro/Getty Images.

Blomquist, Christopher.
Motocross in the X Games / Christopher Blomquist.
    p. cm. — (A kid's guide to the X Games)
Summary: Details the equipment, tricks, and personalities of motocross racing, a new sport at the dangerous X Games.
Includes bibliographical references (p.   ) and index.
  ISBN 0-8239-6303-9 (library binding)
1. Motocross—Juvenile literature. 2. ESPN X-Games—Juvenile literature. [1. Motocross. 2. Motorcycle racing. 3. ESPN X-Games.] I. Title.
  GV1060.12 .B56 2003
  796.7'56—dc21

                                                                        2001007976

Manufactured in the United States of America

Contents

4

As do all motocross riders, Travis Pastrana wears safety gear, including a helmet, nylon pants, and knee-high boots, when he rides his bike.

What Is Motocross?

In the sport called motocross, an **athlete** rides a **lightweight** motorcycle, or motorized bike, up or down ramps. The rider flies through the air on the bike and does tricks in the air. In one of these tricks, a rider kicks his feet over to one side of the bike. In another trick the rider lies down on the bike's seat as if it were a bed. The tricks are sometimes done while the bike is higher than 30 feet (9 m) in the air. That's as tall as five grown-up men standing one on top of another!

Motocross riders are supposed to make smooth landings and not fall off their bikes. This does not always happen. Sometimes the riders crash, and sometimes they hurt themselves. That's why people call motocross an **extreme sport**, or an action sport. Extreme sports always have a lot of action and danger.

Motocross at the X Games

Every summer the extreme sports **competition** known as the summer X Games is held in a U.S. city. At the X Games, the world's best extreme athletes try to win **medals** and prize money. More than $79,000 was awarded in the 2001 summer X Games's three motocross events.

The first summer X Games took place in Rhode Island in 1995. These games had no motocross events. At the time, the sport was still too new and not popular enough to be included. Motocross is the most recent sport to be added to the X Games. It was first run at the 1999 summer X Games in San Francisco, California. That year the freestyle event, in which athletes ride on a dirt **course**, was introduced. The step up event was added in 2000. The big air event, a series of three runs in which each rider gets a turn to jump over a **pit**, was added in 2001.

A rider warms up for the step up event. In this competition, athletes jump over a pole that can be as high as 35 feet (11 m) in the air.

8

Tommy "Tom Cat" Clowers won a motocross medal at the 2000 Summer X Games. This meant he was invited to compete in the next X Games.

Picking Riders for the X Games

A company called LXD Inc. runs the X Games motocross events. LXD also invites the riders to the X Games. So far only men have ever ridden motocross in the X Games. For the freestyle event, the top six riders from the X Games held the year before are invited to compete. The other 10 riders are chosen because they rode well in competitions held by a group called the World Freeriders **Association**, or WFA.

For the step up event, the three best riders from the X Games held the year before are invited. The other 13 invited athletes did well in WFA competitions or in the X Games freestyle event. In 2001, LXD made the first list of invited riders for the new big air event. The list included the top three riders from a tour called the LXD Freeride, seven names chosen by the WFA, and three other riders that LXD thought would be good enough to compete.

Great Moments at the X Games

Tommy "Tom Cat" Clowers, a 27-year-old rider from Santee, California, won the first-ever X-Games motocross step up event in 2000. He also set a world record that day! Clowers jumped over a bar that had been raised 35 feet (11 m) in the air! This was, and still is, the highest anyone had ever jumped in a motocross step up competition. At the location of the event, **Piers** 30–32 in San Francisco, 17,000 fans screamed in excitement when Clowers won.

The next year, at the 2001 summer X Games in Philadelphia, Pennsylvania, star rider Travis Pastrana of Maryland won first place in the freestyle event for the third year in a row. Pastrana, who was 17 years old at the time, now had three gold medals in X-Games motocross. For now, this is the all-time record for motocross gold medals!

Seconds after this photograph of Tommy "Tom Cat" Clowers was taken, thousands of people cheered his record-setting jump.

12

Travis Pastrana watches the big air competition at the 2001 X Games in Philadelphia, Pennsylvania.

Star Riders at the X Games

Travis Pastrana is considered to be the best X-Games motocross rider today. His four summer X-Games medals include gold medals for the freestyle event in 1999, 2000, and 2001, and a second-place silver medal for the step up event in 2001. His tours across the United States sometimes cause him to be away from home for months at a time. Pastrana's parents are often in the crowd when he rides.

Brian Deegan of Canyon Lake, California, also has won four medals in the summer X Games. Deegan is nine years older than Pastrana. He has third-place bronze medals for the 1999 freestyle event and the 2000 freestyle and step up events. Deegan won a second-place silver medal for the big air event in 2001. Deegan likes to look and act tough by wearing black clothes.

The Freestyle Event

The freestyle event takes place on a specially built course that is 300 feet (91m) long by 175 feet (53 m) wide. At the 2001 summer X Games, in Philadelphia, this course was **constructed** in the parking lot of the First Union Center by dumping 275 truckloads of dirt. Fifty workers then shaped that dirt into ramps and hills for the course.

In the freestyle event, there are 16 riders. Each competitor does two 60-second runs. Each rider can score up to 100 points for each run. The riders are judged on how much of the course they use, their style, the tricks they do, and how well they land. The eight best riders make it to the final round. In that round, the riders do two more 60-second runs. Whoever has the best score in the final round wins. At the 1999 X Games, Travis Pastrana ended his first-place run by riding his bike off the course and into San Francisco Bay!

Brian Deegan flies through the air, controlling his bike using only his legs, during the freestyle event at the 2000 summer X Games in San Francisco, California.

15

Tommy "Tom Cat" Clowers is a daring athlete. His bold style has helped him win more step up competitions than any other motocross rider.

The Step Up Event

In the step up event, 16 riders try to jump as high as they can over a **horizontal** pole in the air. Each rider starts 15 to 20 feet (4.5–6 m) away from a dirt mound that is 15 feet (4.5 m) high. Then the rider zooms up the side of the mound and tries to leap over a pole that is several feet in the air over the top of the mound. If the rider's bike hits the pole, he is out of the competition.

After each round, the pole is raised another 6 inches (15 cm). The step up event goes on until there is only one rider **remaining**.

Tommy Clowers has won the summer step up gold medal twice. In 2000, he jumped 35 feet (11 m). In 2001, he jumped 33 feet (10 m).

The Big Air Event

In the big air event, 13 riders have three chances to do their best tricks while flying over a pit that is about 80 feet (24 m) wide. The pit is part of the big air course. The rider races down one ramp and immediately up another ramp. The goal is to get as high in the air as possible over the pit and to do the hardest trick. The best of each rider's three scores is his final one.

At the 2001 summer X Games, Kenny Bartram, a 22-year-old rider from Oklahoma, won the big air gold medal. Bartram is known as Cowboy Kenny. Brian Deegan won the silver medal. That same year, Carey Hart of Nevada broke several bones during the big air event. Hart tried to do the hardest trick of all, a **backflip**, and he crashed. Even today no motocross rider has ever been able to do a backflip on his bike and make a clean landing.

Brian Deegan soars high over the pit in the big air event at the
2001 X Games in Philadelphia, Pennsylvania.

19

A Talk with "Cowboy Kenny" Bartram

What is your favorite X-Games moment?
When Travis Pastrana's score came in at the 2001 big air contest, and it didn't beat my score. That meant that I had for sure won the contest.

How has the X Games changed since you first rode in the competition in 2000?
The biggest change was having room at Philly [Philadelphia]. In San Fran [San Francisco] there were so many people on the pier that you couldn't hardly move. Philly was way better.

How do you prepare a run at the X Games?
I try to treat it just like any other contest. I ride, practice, and figure out what tricks feel better on what jumps, then I sit in the stands and plan out my run. I spend the next couple of hours just going over the run over and over, to make sure that I won't

"Cowboy Kenny" Bartram ▶

forget it while I'm out there. I also go over possibilities of what could go wrong and what I would change if things did take a turn for the worse.

What's your advice to kids who would like to try motocross?
I would just tell them to have fun with it. If you ride just to get famous or make money, it probably won't happen. If you ride because you truly love it or because it is fun to you, then you might.

What's Ahead for Motocross

Motocross is quickly becoming one of the most popular sports at the summer X Games. Motocross is so popular now that a motocross event was even added to the 2001 winter X Games. In this chilly event, the athletes ride their bikes on snow instead of dirt! New motocross events also may be added to the summer X Games. LXD hopes to include a racing event one day. In this event, several motocross athletes would ride on a course at the same time, perform tricks, and race each other to the finish line. Women are also getting in on motocross action. In the fall of 2001, 23-year-old Heidi Henry of Visalia, California, became the first woman to ride in a professional motocross competition. That competition was the MTV Sports and Music Festival in Las Vegas, Nevada. Before too long, women motocross riders probably will have a chance to shine at the X Games, too.

Glossary

association (uh-soh-see-AY-shun) A group of people joined together for a purpose.

athlete (ATH-leet) A person who takes part in sports.

backflip (BAK-flip) A trick where a rider spins upside down in the air on his bike.

competition (kom-peh-TIH-shun) A sports contest.

constructed (kun-STRUKT-id) Built.

course (KOHRS) The track on which motocross competitions are run.

extreme sport (ek-STREEM SPORT) A sport such as motocross, aggressive in-line skating, skateboarding, wakeboarding, bicycle stunt riding, and street luge.

horizontal (hor-ih-ZAHNT-tul) In a side-to-side direction, not up and down.

lightweight (LYT-wayt) Below normal weight.

medals (MEH-dulz) Small, round pieces of metal that are given as awards.

piers (PEERZ) Structures, built out over water, at which boats land.

pit (PIT) A deep hole in the ground.

remaining (ree-MAYN-ing) Left behind.

Index

Web Sites

Due to the changing nature of Internet links, PowerKids Press has developed an online list of Web sites related to the subject of this book. This site is updated regularly. Please use this link to access the list:

www.powerkidslinks.com/kgxg/motoinx/